Flowers

Colouring Book for Adults

Colour and Relax

This colouring book belongs to:

Name: _____

Creative Designe Studio

Thank you for choosing our colouring book.

50 unique flower motifs with different levels of complexity are waiting for you.

Colouring the motifs will not only improve your concentration and motor skills, but will also help you to relax and unwind.

We hope you find a little peace and serenity while colouring our flower pictures.

Have fun!

Let's go!

So, that's it unfortunately...

We hope you had as much fun coloring as we had creating the pictures.

We would be delighted if you leave a positive review on Amazon

😊

You can also look at our other products, maybe there is something for you.

Thank you for your trust in us and the purchase of this coloring book,

your *Creative Designe Studio*

Imprint

Printed in Great Britain
by Amazon